Little BLACK DRESS

From Mourning to Night

Shannon Meyer

Missouri History Museum Press

St. Louis

Distributed by University of Chicago Press

Unless otherwise noted, all dresses and accessories in this book are from the collections of the Missouri Historical Society (which operates the Missouri History Museum). All photos (except page 37) are by Cary Horton.

Library of Congress Cataloging-in-Publication Data
Names: Meyer, Shannon, 1974-
Title: Little black dress : from mourning to night / Shannon Meyer.
Description: St. Louis : Missouri History Museum Press, 2016. |
"Distributed by University of Chicago Press."
Identifiers: LCCN 2015038886 | ISBN 9781883982843 (paperback)
Subjects: LCSH: Dresses--History--Exhibitions. |
Dresses--History--Pictorial
    works--Exhibitions. | Black--Social aspects--History--Exhibitions. |
Color
    in clothing--Social aspects--History--Exhibitions. |
Black--Psychological aspects--History--Exhibitions. |
Mourning customs--History--Exhibitions. |
Fashion--History--Exhibitions. |
Fashion designers--History--Exhibitions.
    | BISAC: DESIGN / Fashion. | HISTORY / General.
Classification: LCC GT2060 .M49 2016 | DDC 391.4/72--dc23
LC record available at http://lccn.loc.gov/2015038886

Cover photos by Cary Horton
Book and cover design by Lauren Mitchell
Distributed by University of Chicago Press
Printed and bound in China by Kings Time Printing Press, Ltd.

Dear Marilyn

The contract we made 62 years ago is still the best contract I've ever made.

Lov ya,

Sam

Contents

One is never overdressed or underdressed with a Little Black Dress.

—Karl Lagerfeld

Introduction

The Missouri Historical Society houses a large and diverse clothing and textile collection of nearly eighteen thousand pieces of men's, women's, and children's clothing, accessories, and household textiles ranging from the late eighteenth century to the present. The Society's primary collecting focus is on items made and worn by St. Louisans. Over the past fifteen years my goal has been to display more objects from this collection through new exhibits. Most of these exhibits have centered on women—their history, their stories, and the clothing they wore throughout their lives. Clothing reveals a lot about a person—everything from a person's physical size to his or her social status. Further research on basic information, such as age, marital status, and number of children the person had, can often add context to the clothing and help explain choices that were made in regard to attire choices at a particular point in a person's life.

When the idea of researching our clothing and textiles for the *Little Black Dress* (or LBD, as it has been affectionately coined) exhibit was brought to my attention several years ago, I was immediately intrigued by the opportunity to showcase both the high-end designer pieces and the everyday department store and homemade dresses that comprise the Society's collection. But I didn't want to stop there. Knowing that the color black had been worn primarily for mourning in the nineteenth century, I felt that the subject of the evolution of the color black from mourning wear to evening wear was a far more fascinating topic. Talking about one point without the other didn't make sense. This turned out to be a harder task than I expected, however: The color black has incredibly complex connotations when it comes to clothing.

When I began looking through the collection for dresses to include in the exhibit, little did I know how many I would actually have to choose from. In fact, I had to make some difficult decisions in eliminating dresses from the artifact list in order to tell the best story that I could on the subject. As I looked through the racks and drawers of dresses, it quickly became apparent that the abundance of black dresses in the collection, covering the entirety of the twentieth century and then some, spoke volumes on the significance of the little black dress to women in this area. Most women purchased their dresses from local stores and dressmakers, whereas others went as far away as Paris to buy or commission a special little black dress made just for them.

Finding mourning clothing to include in the exhibit turned out to be even more of a challenge. I suspect that mourning clothing was worn with some frequency because of Victorian mourning ritual etiquette. Therefore much of it did not survive to be part of our collections. If it did survive, it was often not in the best condition. Furthermore, trying to decipher the intended purpose of a pre-1920s black dress was often difficult. By the late nineteenth century, black worn for mourning was beginning to overlap more frequently with black worn for evening fashions. Without documentation of the original garment owner's use (for example, a second-day wedding dress or a performance dress worn at the World's Fair), research had to be done on family lineage and death dates to determine if the dress was more than likely worn for mourning.

In addition to the evolution of the color black, I tried to explore the complexities and "appropriateness" of the color over time. Black has been used in women's dress throughout history, but the reasons for that have changed. In the sixteenth and seventeenth centuries, European aristocrats used it as a color of power and wealth because achieving a deep, rich black color when dyeing garments was an expensive undertaking. In the eighteenth century, black took a backseat to whites and pastels, but in the nineteenth century it became fashionable again—only this time it was associated with death and despair. Women followed the rules of appropriate Victorian mourning rituals, wearing dull black crepe dresses for nearly a century. Toward the end of the nineteenth century, women began to choose luxurious black silks and velvets for evening wear, but it was considered an inappropriate color for younger, unmarried women because of its impure connotations. Further, wearing black undergarments outside of mourning was considered incredibly risqué.

With the roles changing for women during World War I, mourning customs became impractical and old-fashioned. By the mid-1920s, black was considered modern, and Coco Chanel's little black dress became a "uniform of the modern woman" (French *Vogue*, 1926). Black quickly gained social acceptance for "mature" women in everyday dress throughout the twentieth century. By the 1960s, black was taken over by the youth, and it was often associated with rebellion.

Today most people still consider it appropriate to wear black and dark colors for funerals, but black knows no bounds and is considered socially acceptable for all occasions and ages. For decades now, the LBD has become an essential item in almost every woman's wardrobe and has proven to be the perfect go-to outfit. Many people, from fashion designers to housewives, have used their talents and personal aesthetic to create their own version of the perfect little black dress. And though we may not always know who wore the dresses in this exhibit, they speak to women of all ages, races, and backgrounds. From the deep shroud of mourning to the mannequin in a boutique, and from cocktail hour to the high school prom, these dresses help to tell the story of a complex color and the designers and women who love it.

There are many people whose hard work made this exhibit possible. Special thanks go to former and current Missouri Historical Society staff members Cailin Carter, Shery Hunter, Diane Riley, Katie Moon, and intern Illana Moreno for their help very early in the process. My deep gratitude and thanks also go to interns Kami Ahrens and Aviana Brown, whose help and dedication to this project at its most critical time proved invaluable. Special thanks also goes to staff photographer Cary Horton for the beautiful pictures throughout the exhibit's companion catalog, and to exhibition designer Nicole Gray D'Orazio for working to shape this story into a beautiful exhibit.

Mourning Traditions

The color black has long been associated with funerals and the practice of mourning loved ones. Western mourning traditions began when early Christians adapted pagan practices into religious funeral rites. Black clothing, originally worn to hide the living from the dead, was used instead to reflect the suffering of the soul. Funeral rites grew more elaborate during the Renaissance period and were indicative of wealth and affluence. Restrictive fashion codes called sumptuary laws were put in place to prevent lower classes from emulating the funeral customs of the upper classes. These barriers began to break down as the middle class grew in the following centuries.

At the beginning of the nineteenth century a new feeling of romanticism and sentimentality regarding death became prevalent. When Prince Albert of Britain died in 1861, women of all classes followed the example of Queen Victoria, who plunged into deep mourning for her husband. Her position as a figurehead and international role model glamourized mourning, resulting in a cultlike obsession. Strict social rules developed, outlining the exact color, fabrics, and length of time to be used in mourning. Ladies' fashion magazines helped disseminate this information by publishing fashion plates and articles on mourning etiquette. The demand for mourning wear and accessories grew so high during this time that mourning warehouses were established to sell ready-made items. Women who couldn't afford to buy new clothes could chemically dye their clothing black at home.

The Victorian cult of mourning continued until World War I. New roles for women emerged, gradually erasing elaborate mourning rituals. Though people continued to wear black and dark colors for funerals (and do so even today) the etiquette became impractical, and the required stages of grieving and isolation were shortened, slowly becoming obsolete. By the 1920s, people were able to wear black clothing regularly without the association of mourning.

Degrees of Mourning

During the Victorian era there arose strict social rules for women outlining the degrees of mourning. Each of these stages—deepest or full mourning, second mourning, and half mourning—required specific amounts of time and certain attire. In the deepest stage of mourning, women wore dull black dresses made from crepe, wool, or broadcloth. Widows spent one year and one day in this stage, but the period was shorter when mourning other family members. Grieving mothers accessorized with white to reflect the purity of their children. Second mourning allowed some non-black trim and slight variation on accessories and lasted nine months for widows. Women grieving for a sibling spent six months in this stage. Half mourning was much more relaxed than the previous two periods. Women could introduce some color—any shade of gray, lavender, or mauve—and include subtle patterns. This final stage lasted six months to life for widows.

Men and children were also required to partake in mourning, but not to the same degree as women. Men were generally obligated to wear a black armband or hatband for the deceased, and children under age twelve wore black or they wore white with a black sash or trimmings. Women were held responsible for representing their family's wealth, respectability, and morality, forcing them to adhere to more rigorous mourning practices than men and children.

$\mathscr{T}$his dress was likely worn during a time of full mourning. The coarsely woven fabric presents a dull surface, and the accompanying trim is simple and inconspicuous. Despite deepest mourning generally calling for simplicity of dress, the fashionable silhouette and style of the time period were still often adhered to.

Two-piece wool crepe mourning dress,
ca. 1904
Unknown maker
Gift of Mrs. J. W. Hager
1985 065 0069

*B*ecause this dress is plain black crepe with subtle white trim, it could represent the first stage of mourning for a mother who lost a child, or the second stage of mourning for other relations, when grief was lessened slightly and small appearances of non-black embellishments were allowed.

TWO-PIECE SILK AND CREPE MOURNING
DRESS WITH ORGANDY TRIM,
CA. 1875
UNKNOWN MAKER
1985 065 0047

*E*liza Albray Wessel wore this dress when mourning one, or both, of her parents. Her mother, Sarah Fearing Cushman Albray, died in 1868, and her father, John Albray, in 1871. At the time of their deaths Eliza was living in Cincinnati with her husband, Augustus Wessel, and four children. She later moved to St. Louis to live with her daughter Mina and Mina's husband, Alfred Lee Shapleigh, who was secretary and treasurer of Shapleigh Hardware Company.

The high luster of the dress may seem inappropriate for mourning, but moiré was a fabric commonly sold by retailers for mourning purposes.

TWO-PIECE SILK MOIRÉ
MOURNING DRESS, 1867–1871
UNKNOWN MAKER
GIFT OF JANE SHAPLEIGH KERCHEVAL
1966 010 0004

$\mathcal{T}$his dress was worn by either Emily Rose or Ida Rose Uhri when mourning the loss of their father, German doctor Carl Frederick Edward Rose. Dr. Rose had immigrated to St. Louis in 1840 at the suggestion of Mr. Catlin of St. Louis, whom he had met while practicing medicine in Hanover, Germany.

In second mourning, women were allowed to decorate their dresses with jet beading and other details. The design of this bodice and skirt reveals the heavy influence of contemporary fashion on mourning wear.

TWO-PIECE FAILLE MOURNING DRESS
WITH JET BEADING, CA. 1890
UNKNOWN MAKER
GIFT OF MRS. JAMES A. MARITZ JR.
1984 094 0006

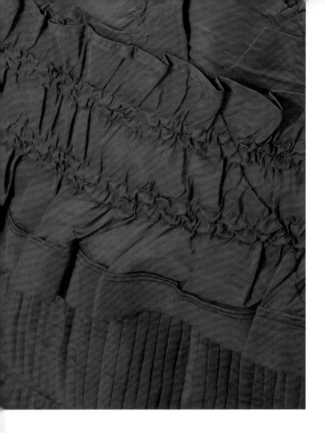

*I*n half mourning—the third and final stage—women could introduce some color back into their dress. Shades of gray, purple, lavender, or mauve were considered acceptable, as was the inclusion of subtle patterns.

This dress, worn by Emma Elise Wernse, dates to the early 1880s. Emma's father had died in 1880, and this lavender dress would have been appropriate for her final stage of mourning. Mourning the loss of a parent generally lasted for eighteen months, regardless of whether the child was young or grown.

Two-piece silk taffeta dress, ca. 1882
Unknown maker
Gift of C. D. Depew
1964 062 0001

To weep is to make less the depth of grief.

— William Shakespeare

Expressions of Grief

Certain accessories were associated with mourning. Bottles of this shape were sometimes used for perfume, but they were also used to collect the tears of the grieving. The use of tear catchers, also known as lacrimatories, began in the Roman Empire. The amount of tears collected was thought to reflect the status of the deceased. During the Victorian era these bottles once again rose in popularity for both men and women. The rim of the bottle was designed to fit underneath the eye to aid in the catching of tears, while the interior was funneled to collect them. Some bottles were sealed; others were left open to let the tears evaporate. Some believed that once the tears evaporated, the mourning period was over.

GLASS LACRIMATORY OR PERFUME BOTTLE, 1904
UNKNOWN MAKER
GIFT OF WILLIAM E. PIEBER
2009 052 1675

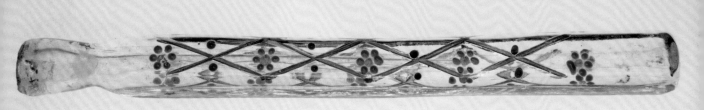

*J*ewelry created to remember or honor an individual often was made with hair because it is a personal, lightweight artifact that does not degrade over time. Hair jewelry was used as a token of love in the 1500s but transitioned to a relic of mourning during the 1800s. Young women usually made the jewelry, using self-instruction manuals such as Mark Campbell's *The Art of Hair Work*. These publications provided tutorials, designs, and catalogs of materials needed to produce elaborate hair jewelry. Hair could also be sent, along with payment, to companies that would create the jewelry and send it back. However, the integrity of this method, in regard to whose hair was actually being used and returned, was questionable, so many women created craft circles to prepare their own hair work.

NECKLACE MADE OF HAIR WITH
HEART-SHAPED PENDANT, 1850–1880
UNKNOWN MAKER
GIFT OF MRS. W. R. SWAIN
1959 001 0039

This set of hair jewelry includes a brooch, earrings, and a bracelet. The brooch incorporates symbols of acorns and grape leaves. In mourning, acorns represented the end of a long life. Grape leaves were intended to reflect the Christian faith. These symbols are repeated in the earrings. The bracelet closes with a buckle, which was intended to represent close bonds of either friendship or romance.

BROOCH, EARRINGS, AND BRACELET SET
MADE OF HAIR, CA. 1880
UNKNOWN MAKER
GIFT OF MRS. WESLEY R. MELLOW AND
MRS. GEORGE E. MELLOW
1960 086 0001–0003

$\mathcal{J}$et, a stone created naturally from fossilized driftwood, rose in popularity during the middle of the nineteenth century. Historically, jet had been used as a charm to ward against magic and danger, but it became a Christian symbol in the Middle Ages. The dark, dull appearance of the stone made it an ideal mourning accessory. The most sought-after jet came from Whitby, England, but demand in the Victorian era outstripped the natural supply. Imitation jet was created from alternate substances, such as glass or vulcanite, an early form of plastic. These false forms of jet were less expensive and more common throughout the latter half of the nineteenth century.

JET NECKLACE, CA. 1875 (LEFT)
UNKNOWN MAKER
1985 003 0003

IMITATION JET NECKLACE, CA. 1860 (RIGHT)
UNKNOWN MAKER
GIFT OF J. BOYD HILL
1967 067 0001

In 1874 the Fowler Brothers of Providence, Rhode Island, began manufacturing English crepe stone. This black and dull stone perfectly fit the bill for mourning jewelry. Crepe stone, named for its similarity to the fabric texture, is made from onyx treated with acids to produce a wrinkled appearance. Crepe stone can also be produced from molded glass. These bracelets were patented only five years after crepe stone was introduced.

CREPE STONE BRACELETS, CA. 1879
UNKNOWN MAKER
GIFT OF NEWELL AUGER
1965 098 0000

$\mathcal{O}$riginating from at least the sixteenth century, fede rings were originally used to symbolize a marriage contract. The style of two clasped hands takes its name from the phrase *mani in fede*, Italian for "hands in faith." The symbol was incorporated into mourning wear to remember loved ones and show loyalty to the departed. Rings were commonly distributed among the family of the deceased.

MOURNING FEDE RING, 1850–1900
UNKNOWN MAKER
GIFT OF MRS. JOHN E. CONRADES
1983 097 0001

This mourning brooch was made to memorialize Charles and Agnes Woodson, who died in 1785 and 1796, respectively. The woman pictured next to the tomb is believed to be their daughter Caroline Matilda Bates, mother of the second Missouri governor, Frederick Bates. A weeping willow is used to signify grief and sorrow, while the urn on top of the tomb represents a vessel for the soul.

MOURNING BROOCH IN MEMORY OF AGNES
AND CHARLES WOODSON, 1796
UNKNOWN MAKER
GIFT OF CAROL BATES
1953 123 0001

Women think of all colors except the absence of color. I have said that black has it all. White too. Their beauty is absolute. It is the perfect harmony.

—Coco Chanel

Black in Early Fashion

Associated with everything from evil to melancholy to luxury and sophistication, black is a complicated color to categorize—particularly when it comes to dress. Between the late nineteenth and early twentieth centuries, people wore black for both mourning and fashion. Fabric choices and trims helped to distinguish between the two: dull crepe versus satin, jet versus sequins.

Before Chanel helped to popularize the color black for everyday fashion in the 1920s, women wore black for a variety of reasons. Outside of mourning, some women wore black for work situations. The uniforms of maids and shopkeepers were often black—though the black associated with women's work was often dull and modest. Some women wore black for practicality, helping to hide the dirt and grime of everyday life in industrialized cities. Some women wore black for sport: The equestrian riding clothing of the late nineteenth century was styled after men's clothing with a bodice and skirt in black wool, as well as a black top hat and riding boots. And still others, particularly women of means, began wearing black for fashionable evening wear once again. In previous centuries achieving a rich, deep black color was expensive, reserved primarily for the upper class and royalty—thus giving it more of an appeal to wealthy women as a symbol of status. Black evening wear was dramatic and mysterious. It was also regarded as seductive and powerful. Because of this, for many years it was considered a more appropriate choice for married and older women.

The turning point for wearing black in everyday life came during World War I, when entire nations were in mourning for the indelible loss of lives, and black became the dominant color in fashion. It was also during this time that the concept of the "little black dress" emerged, as fabric usage was scaled back to aid the war effort.

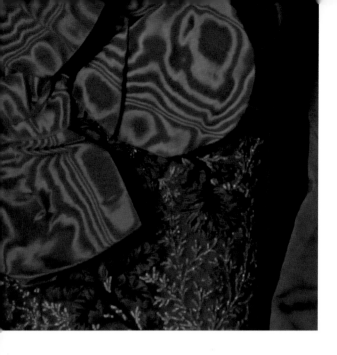

This fashionable black dress from the 1880s was custom made in New York for Julia Maffitt Walsh around the time of her marriage to Edward Walsh Jr., a prominent businessman and president of the Mississippi Glass Company. Julia Maffitt was born into a wealthy St. Louis family of significant standing in 1855, her father a doctor for the U.S. Army and her mother the great-granddaughter of St. Louis's founding father Auguste Chouteau. Though it could have doubled as a mourning dress, it is believed that this may have been part of Maffitt's wedding trousseau. Asymmetrical draping, pleats, and long trains (for evening wear) were very typical of dress styles in the 1880s, as well as a large bustle.

Two-piece silk and silk faille moiré
evening dress, ca. 1880
Made by Josephine G. Egan, New York
Gift of Julia Maffitt Lamy, Mary Lamy
Phillips, and Isabel Lamy Lee
1988 098 0005

$\mathcal{W}$ith its modest appearance one might think this dress more appropriate for mourning than celebrating. However, this dress was worn by Ettie Lenora Ansell McCollester as a second-day dress, which was donned the day after one's wedding to attend events and celebrations.

Ettie Ansell married farmer George Alfred McCollester in 1895. The couple lived in California, Missouri, and had six children. A picture of Ettie in her second-day dress (above, by Coopers Studio; in the collections of the Missouri Historical Society) shows that some minor alterations have been made to the frock: The black-beaded trim on the lapel and standup collar has been removed, black lace on the shoulders has been removed, and a white bow-like ornament attached to the center of the collar is also gone. The removal of the trim could have been an effort to update the dress or to transfer it to another dress. The tightly cinched waist and large leg-of-mutton sleeves were the height of fashion in the 1890s.

TWO-PIECE SECOND-DAY DRESS, 1895
UNKNOWN MAKER
GIFT OF MARY ANN GROETSCH
2014 142 0001

$\mathcal{G}$irolamo Giuseffi, owner of G. Giuseffi Ladies' Tailoring Company, was a highly reputable dressmaker in the St. Louis area in the 1900s. An Italian immigrant, Giuseffi moved to St. Louis at the end of the nineteenth century after working for a dressmaker in Boston. Upon his arrival, he opened his own shop on Olive Street and quickly became successful. Giuseffi's business expanded after more of his family was able to immigrate to the United States. His two sisters worked as cutters and fitters, but Giuseffi remained the primary designer. He drew inspiration from the latest Parisian fashions as well as those from New York, but he was known for his elaborate designs and decorations. He moved his business to Westminster Place around 1905 and opened his famous "Gold Room," where customers would wait to be fitted. His reputation expanded his popularity and earned him recognition across the country.

This dress is believed to have belonged to Elizabeth Boyd Kennard, granddaughter of Augustus Frederick Shapleigh of the St. Louis hardware store A. F. Shapleigh & Company and wife of John Burton Kennard, president of a St. Louis carpet company. It would have been worn for evening events such as dinners or receptions.

TWO-PIECE SILK TAFFETA DRESS, CA. 1904
MADE BY G. GIUSEFFI LADIES' TAILORING
COMPANY, ST. LOUIS
GIFT OF MRS. ROLLA WELLS STREET
1980 018 0001

38

$\mathcal{I}$n the early 1900s, dresses were made to fit the popular silhouette of the S-bend curve. This look was achieved by the use of a "health corset" that forced the wearer's hips back and bosom forward into an awkward S-shaped bend. The intention of the corset was to relieve pressure on the stomach, although the position it forced the wearer to stand and walk in offset any healthy side effects. The corset sat lower on the body, creating a dropped, monobosom appearance referred to as a pouter pigeon silhouette for its resemblance to the bird.

Alma Borman owned this pouter pigeon style dress in 1904. She was a singer from Chicago who wore this dress while performing at the 1904 World's Fair in St. Louis.

TWO-PIECE BLACK NET EVENING DRESS
TRIMMED WITH SEQUINS AND BEADS, 1904
UNKNOWN MAKER
GIFT OF P. JAYNES
1950 104 0001

$\mathscr{D}$uring World War I, black fell out of favor for mourning because almost everyone suffered losses. Instead, black became part of everyday wardrobes. Many women joined the workforce, which was reflected in their clothing. The impractical corset began to disappear, and fashion designers created new styles with a higher waist and natural bustline. Hemlines rose slightly, and tailored clothing and suits became the preferred silhouette. This tulle and lace dress reflects those changes with its lower neckline, less confining design, and shorter hem.

Silk evening dress with tulle
and lace overlay, ca. 1918
Unknown maker
Gift of Isabelle E. Burton
1986 059 0006

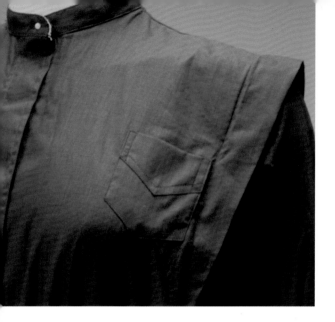

Black at Work

With industrialization and the rapid growth of cities in the nineteenth century, the black suit became the fashionable "uniform" of the urban working man. This was serious black—successful black. However, for women who needed to work outside the home, there were very few acceptable jobs and even fewer professional positions, mostly as factory workers or maids and governesses. The uniform of domestic work became the simple black dress, but unlike successful and enterprising men's clothing, or elegant and sophisticated women's high fashion, this was dull black—modest black, the black that helped to hide the dirt and grime of life in the city.

This uniform was made by Dix-Make and sold at Stix, Baer and Fuller, a St. Louis retailer that opened its doors on Washington Avenue in 1892. Dix-Make specialized in nurse and maid uniforms. The simple black cotton dress would have been most appropriate for wear by a household servant.

COTTON UNIFORM DRESS, CA. 1910
MADE BY DIX-MAKE, NEW YORK
GIFT OF THE ESTATE OF
RICHARD LOCKWOOD
X09390

Simplicity is the keynote of all true elegance.

—Coco Chanel

Coco Chanel and the Little Black Dress

Gabrielle Chanel was born to an impoverished family in France in 1883 and sent to an orphanage when she was just twelve years old, following her mother's death. There, she learned to sew, which enabled her to find work as a seamstress after leaving the orphanage. Originally aspiring to a career in music, she sang at a cabaret in the evenings where she earned the nickname "Coco."

With financial assistance, Chanel was able to open her first shop, Chanel Modes, in 1910, where she worked as a milliner. By 1913 she added a line of knit sportswear, which went against the grain of the restricting fashions of the time. Her designs made a huge impact in liberating women from the constraints of their corsets. Obsessed with comfort and proper fit, many of Chanel's garments were made of jersey, a comfortable and practical fabric that at the time was typically used for undergarments. By 1919 her success allowed her to move to a larger building on the Rue Cambon, where the couture House of Chanel is still located today. Chanel introduced her trademark collarless jackets in 1925 and gained notoriety for her little black dresses in 1926. Her personal style, financial independence, and exquisite taste made her a model for modern women around the world. Chanel closed her shop during World War II but made a successful comeback in 1953 at the age of seventy. Her re-entry into fashion was an effort to save women from Christian Dior's "New Look" of tight waists and full skirts—a look she found too repressive for modern women. Her success continued until her death in 1971.

Coco Chanel's designs are considered timeless, and she herself is a style icon. In 1999 she was the only fashion designer listed in *Time* magazine's "100 Most Influential People of the Twentieth Century."

The October 1, 1926, issue of American *Vogue* magazine featured a small illustration of a black Chanel dress. Comparing it to the reliable and only-available-in-black Model-T car, *Vogue* wrote, "The Chanel 'Ford,' the frock that all the world will wear, is model 817 of black crepe de chine. The bodice blouses slightly at the front and sides and has a tight bolero at the back. Especially chic is the arrangement of tiny tucks which cross in front. Imported by Saks." The simple unadorned dress caused little excitement in the fashion world, especially with American women, though French *Vogue* later called the dress the "uniform of the modern woman" (November 1926).

Coco Chanel's "little black dress," *Vogue*, October 1, 1926. Courtesy of Condé Nast.

$\mathcal{T}$he "Gabrielle Chanel" tag in this dress helps to date it to around 1919, and it is an early example of Chanel's simple and comfortable style, as well as her use of black. Though recognition of her "little black dress" didn't come until the mid-1920s, some of her earliest designs were in black, opposed to the bright colors so popular of the time period. Chanel preferred neutral colors; her use of black only increased after the death of her lover, Arthur "Boy" Capel in 1919.

The style of this dress is indicative of the era, with its tubular shape, free-hanging front panel, and accented waistline. Chanel began her first couture collection in 1916, adding fur-trimmed pieces in 1918 and black velvet capes trimmed with ostrich in 1919. This dress came with a black velvet fur-trimmed cape.

VELVET DAY DRESS, CA. 1919
MADE BY CHANEL, PARIS
1985 065 0017

Chanel generally kept her designs simple and modern. This lace dress features the "shoestring" shoulder straps that Chanel helped to popularize, as well as the shorter hem length, falling just below the knee, that began around 1925. The dress was purchased October 22, 1928, by Elsie Rauh for 4,320 francs, the equivalent of almost US $900 (approximately $12,000 today). Elsie was the wife of Aaron Rauh, vice president of Rice-Stix Dry Goods Company in St. Louis. Rice-Stix was one of St. Louis's largest importers and wholesale dealers of foreign and domestic dry goods.

LACE EVENING DRESS WITH
CREPE DE CHINE UNDERDRESS, 1928
MADE BY CHANEL, PARIS
GIFT OF MRS. HENRY SCHERCK
1982 005 0001

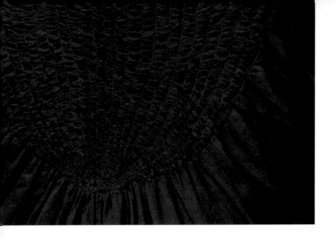

$\mathcal{C}$hanel continued to use black throughout her career, as it was central to her design philosophy and aesthetic. In the 1930s, as women's styles became more elegant and sophisticated, Chanel was at the height of her popularity—employing four thousand people and dressing everyone from wealthy housewives to Hollywood starlets.

This elegant chiffon evening dress was worn by Mary Elizabeth Lumaghi. Mary was born in 1905, the daughter of Louis F. and Laura Green Lumaghi. Her father operated the Lumaghi Coal Company of Collinsville, Illinois. Mary graduated from Mary Institute—then a division of Washington University—in 1923 and from Smith College in Massachusetts in 1927. After college Mary was an active member of the Junior League of St. Louis and worked for a time as a medical receptionist. In 1939 she married James Marsh Douglas, a justice of the Missouri Supreme Court, and moved to Jefferson City. Her son, James Kimball, was born there in 1942. In 1949 the family returned to St. Louis upon Judge Douglas's retirement from the bench to become a senior partner of law firm Thompson, Mitchell, Thompson and Douglas. According to her son, Mary "happily served as a housewife, mother and, consonant with her husband's stature in the legal and political communities, a gracious hostess."

SLEEVELESS CHIFFON EVENING DRESS
WITH SHIRRED BODICE, CA. 1935
MADE BY CHANEL, PARIS
GIFT OF JAMES KIMBALL DOUGLAS
1975 005 0002

You can wear black at any time. You can wear it at any age. You may wear it on almost any occasion. A little black frock is essential to a woman's wardrobe. I could write a book about black.

— *Christian Dior*

Black and Everyday Versatility

After World War I, black become a regular feature in women's wardrobes. In 1922, etiquette author Emily Post stated "nothing really can compare with the utility and smartness of black" (*Etiquette in Society, in Business, in Politics and at Home*, 1922). By the 1930s all major couture designers featured black dresses in their collections, each adding their own touches to create their version of the little black dress. By the 1950s, black had become the go-to color for women, as both black suits and dresses became favored for cocktail parties. The color was taken over by the younger generation in the 1960s as designers began making black clothing marketed toward teenagers and young women. By the 1980s many designers were emphasizing the practicality of black, focusing on fashions for the working woman.

For the last century the black dress has proven to be the most versatile piece of clothing a woman can own. It can be dressed up or down, worn to work, and then out to dinner. Changing the accessories can alter the appearance of the dress. Every woman should own a versatile little black dress.

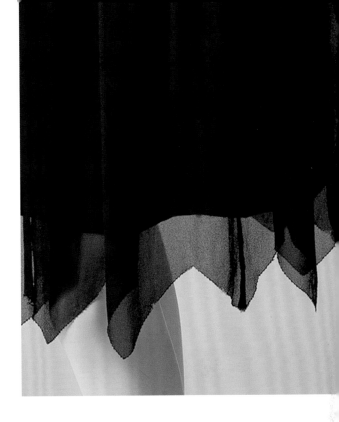

The 1920s brought about the era of the youthful, active woman. As clothing became more casual, the previous generations' notions of propriety based on the occasion or even the time of day became far more relaxed. Hemlines and sleeves crept up, and women started shaving their legs and underarms, plucking their eyebrows, cutting their hair, and wearing makeup.

The popular fashion mode dictated by girls in their late teens and twenties was straight and flat, achieved by wearing loose-fitting dresses, which fell in a straight line from the shoulders, barely touching the body. This dress was worn by Irene Dost Locker, who would have been twenty years old in 1925. The uneven hemline was popular in both evening wear and day dresses.

SLEEVELESS CREPE DRESS, CA. 1925
UNKNOWN MAKER
GIFT OF JOAN SHEPPARD
2006 186 0057

$\mathcal{W}$hile the clothing of the 1920s was comparatively more simple than in years before, the design and decoration was often complicated and ornate. The use of geometric forms became popular, such as the check pattern of this dress. Decorative stitching, buttons, pleats, tucks, and ruching were just some of the elaborate design elements used during this period. This dress also features decorative pocket flaps with satin ball trim, as well as pleated crepe ruffles.

CREPE-BACK SATIN DRESS, 1925–1930
UNKNOWN MAKER
1985 065 0016

$\mathcal{B}$etween 1929 and 1930, styles changed fairly abruptly as the shorter hemlines and baggy dresses of the youth-centered flapper culture disappeared and a more mature look came into style. Hemlines grew longer, and the bust and waist reappeared as the trend moved toward more femininity in fashion. Fashions emphasized a tall, thin silhouette with broad shoulders and a more natural waistline, all of which can be seen in these two dresses. Both were owned by Claire Marie Bacon Hagee of St. Louis, who would have been in her forties when she wore them.

LEFT: SHORT-SLEEVE CREPE DRESS WITH
BUTTON-FRONT CLOSURE, CA. 1935
UNKNOWN MAKER
GIFT OF GEORGE B. HAGEE
2001 170 0007

RIGHT: SHORT-SLEEVE RAYON CREPE DRESS
WITH BEADED COLLAR AND CUFFS, CA. 1937
UNKNOWN MAKER
GIFT OF GEORGE B. HAGEE
2001 170 0006

Doris Dodson

Doris Dodson, a junior-wear company, was located at 1120 Washington Avenue in downtown St. Louis. The label was created by Forest City Manufacturing Company in fall 1936, a few years after Irving Sorger introduced junior-size clothing. Sorger, a manager for Kline's in St. Louis, recognized the need among teenage girls for their own, more youthful styles and sizes. He enlisted help from fashion design students at Washington University in St. Louis and started a trend that spread across the nation. Taking the lead, St. Louis designers introduced hundreds of new junior-wear lines. Doris Dodson was one of at least ten manufacturers located downtown on Washington. Designers such as Grace Davile and Alice Topp-Lee worked for the company before it closed in 1968.

This rayon dress with a fitted bodice and short, puffed sleeves was made for the junior market, which meant the sizing included a slightly higher chest, a shorter waist, and a smaller waistline. Though the junior dresses were intended for younger women, older women sometimes wore dresses in junior sizes because they liked the fit.

JUNIOR BLACK RAYON DRESS WITH NET YOKE
AND VELVET TRIM, CA. 1938
MADE BY DORIS DODSON, ST. LOUIS
GIFT OF HARRIS E. WILLIAMS
1996 391 0001

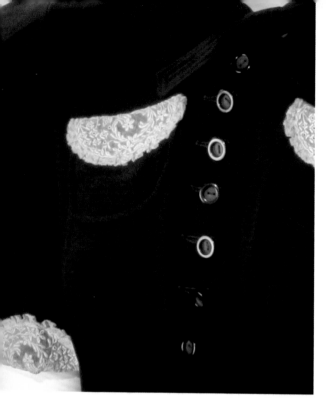

*B*etween 1930 and 1946, styles for women remained relatively unchanged, with the exception of slightly shorter, fuller skirts beginning in the late 1930s. Wartime restrictions and rationing began in 1942, and the shortage of materials limited the widths of skirts and the availability of fine fabrics. Women were often forced to refashion their old clothing at home, and rayon was often used as a substitute for silk.

Throughout this time period, Parisian couture designer Elsa Schiaparelli continued to popularize the color black in fashion by pairing it with contrasting colors like pink and green. The maker of this dress followed that trend by using simple contrasting white lace to add a more sophisticated touch.

RAYON CREPE DRESS WITH SCALLOPED
LACE TRIM, CA. 1940
UNKNOWN MAKER
GIFT OF ROBERT L. AND
ROSE M. BRODERICK ESTATE
2004 046 0007

Maternity Wear

Post–World War II stability and prosperity resulted in a baby boom that put a new focus on maternity clothes for women. Advertised as "cool, comfortable and smart," Smink maternity clothes were available at retail shops and boutiques throughout the country in the 1940s and ranged in price from $27.50 to $39.95. This dress has a snap on each side, as well as built-in ties at the back to help control the amount of fullness needed throughout a pregnancy.

RAYON CREPE MATERNITY DRESS WITH
CRISSCROSS TIES AT NECK AND AN
EXPANDABLE WAIST, CA. 1945
MADE BY SMINK MATERNITY CLOTHES
1991 029 0002

Traina-Norell

After World War II, many women were happily returning to a more feminine look when French designer Christian Dior revealed his "New Look" collection in 1947. The must-have silhouette for women returned to a full skirt with cinched waist, rounded hips, and small shoulders. These dresses, made by American designer Norman Norell, follow the new silhouette.

Born in Noblesville, Indiana, Norell began his career at Hattie Carnegie before teaming with wholesale clothing manufacturer Anthony Traina in 1941 to make high-end clothing for the mature and sophisticated woman. Considered a leading American fashion designer throughout the 1940s and 1950s, Norell translated French couture fashions for the ready-to-wear market with precise fit and quality. He won the first Coty American Fashion Critics' Award in 1943, an award created to promote American fashion designers during World War II.

This dress was worn by Millie Fabick, co-founder of Fleur de Lis in St. Louis, a Catholic social organization created for high school students in 1958 that also raises money for Cardinal Glennon Children's Medical Center. Fabick's addition of a large white lace collar and matching cuffs alters the look of the dress, giving it a more modest appearance.

BELTED TAFFETA DRESS WITH ADDED LACE
COLLAR AND CUFFS, CA. 1949
MADE BY TRAINA-NORELL, NEW YORK
GIFT OF MRS. FRANCIS J. FABICK
1968 044 0000

Though the idea of cocktail hour began as early as the 1920s, the cocktail party became all the rage in the 1950s, and with it came certain standards of dress. The cocktail dress was appropriate for late-afternoon or early evening events, was often black, and was generally made of silks or satins, finer fabrics than those used in day wear. Cocktail dresses were shorter than the more formal floor-length evening wear and were accessorized with the proper hat, gloves, and jewelry.

TAFFETA COCKTAIL DRESS, CA. 1948
MADE BY TRAINA-NORELL, NEW YORK
GIFT OF MRS. WILLIAM J. WESSELING
1978 061 0003

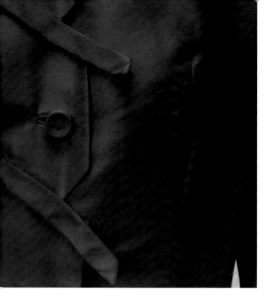

Hattie Carnegie

Ten years after immigrating to New York from Austria, Hattie Carnegie opened her first hat and dress shop in 1909, despite not knowing how to sew. By 1918 she had bought out her partner and began hiring young designers such as Norman Norell, Pauline Trigère, James Galanos, and Claire McCardell to create her designs. She continued to produce hats and dresses, as well as jewelry, creating an empire worth over $6 million. She wanted her clothing to be simple, move well, and show off the wearer. After her death in 1956 the label continued producing custom dresses until 1965 and accessories until 1976.

This silk faille dress exemplifies Hattie Carnegie's aesthetic with its simple shirtwaist design, Bermuda collar, and figure-flattering waistline made with darts. The four placard "tabs" down the center are a unique design element.

SILK FAILLE DRESS WITH CENTER-FRONT
PLACARD TABS, CA. 1950
MADE BY HATTIE CARNEGIE, NEW YORK
GIFT OF WILLIAM K. SULLIVAN
1993 014 0056

Nat Kaplan

Nat Kaplan started manufacturing dresses in New York in 1935. Though not as well known as other designers from this time period, Kaplan made ready-to-wear dresses that were finely tailored and cost slightly more than other labels. When Kaplan died unexpectedly in 1956, his wife, Sylvia, took over the business. A single mother of four children, Sylvia ran the business successfully with her son Richard until 1986. She also acted as the fit model and insisted that all of the clothing produced be flattering, comfortable, and easy to wear.

This silk satin dress worn by Virginia Kinet has overlapping front bodice panels with decorative buttons. The fullness of the skirt is controlled with large figure-flattering pleats at the waist.

SILK SATIN DRESS WITH OVERLAPPING
FRONT BODICE PANELS AND
THREE-QUARTER-LENGTH SLEEVES, CA. 1951
MADE BY NAT KAPLAN, NEW YORK
GIFT OF MS. VIRGINIA KINET
1976 042 0006

This simple, yet feminine, dress was worn by Erna E. Postel in the early 1950s. Erna and her sister Alma married brothers Urban and Allan Postel in 1911. Erna and Urban lived in Mascoutah, Illinois, with their four children. This dress features alternating strips of cotton and satin fabric with a belted bow at the waist. Erna may have made this dress herself, as she was a gifted seamstress and quilter. While much of the family's clothing was donated to the Missouri Historical Society, two of her quilts are in the collection of the Art Institute of Chicago.

SHORT-SLEEVE COTTON DRESS WITH
SATIN STRIPES, CA. 1953
UNKNOWN MAKER
GIFT OF BERNICE A. POSTEL
2002 078 0032

Ceil Chapman

New York designer Ceil Chapman began her first company in 1940 with the help of Gloria Vanderbilt, then later went into business with her husband. Although she had no formal training in design, she was very adept at intricate draping, tucking, and folding of fabric, creating engineered designs. Chapman dressed movie stars like Elizabeth Taylor and Marilyn Monroe, but she still managed to make dresses that were affordable to the public, selling in boutiques and department stores.

This black silk crepe dress was worn by former Missouri Historical Society curator Cay Judah in the 1950s. The shirred bodice and pencil skirt create a fitted silhouette, to accentuate a full bosom and hips. The tight pencil skirt became popular in the 1950s, a direct contrast to the voluminous full skirt popular at the same time. Because of its suggestive nature, it was considered inappropriate for younger girls.

SILK CREPE DRESS WITH GATHERED BODICE
AND SHAWL COLLAR, CA. 1955
MADE BY CEIL CHAPMAN, NEW YORK
GIFT OF MR. AND MRS. ROBERT M. JUDAH
1969 031 0165

Maternity Wear

Even in pregnancy women want to maintain a level of fashion, and black has always been a "slimming" color. This polyester knit dress was worn by Joan Sheppard during the second trimesters of her pregnancies in the 1960s. Both the trapeze shape and scalloped collar resembling flower petals give the dress an innocent and childlike appearance, which was a very popular aesthetic in the mid- to late 1960s.

Donor Joan Sheppard attended college at the University of Illinois Urbana–Champaign, where she met her husband, Charles. They married in 1953 and built a house in Godfrey, Illinois, where they reared four children. Joan has served as a member, board member, or executive committee member for more than fifty organizations over the years.

POLYESTER KNIT MATERNITY DRESS WITH
SCALLOPED COLLAR, CA. 1959–1965
UNKNOWN MAKER
GIFT OF JOAN L. SHEPPARD
2006 186 0041

Jane Franklin Juniors

Jane Franklin Juniors was just one of the many companies specializing in the junior-wear market that started in St. Louis in the 1930s. This dress reflects the more restrained fashions of the early 1960s, before the heyday of the miniskirt and A-line dresses. This wool jersey dress features an unusual attached front panel that extends from the neckline, wraps around the waist, and buttons at the back like a belt.

WOOL JERSEY DRESS WITH
THREE-QUARTER-LENGTH SLEEVES,
CA. 1960–1966
MADE BY JANE FRANKLIN JUNIORS, ST. LOUIS
1993 014 0008

𝒴outhful designs dominated women's clothing in the mid- to late 1960s. British designer Mary Quant popularized the miniskirt, and dresses were often childlike with bright colors and psychedelic prints. Similar to the 1920s, the general style reflected that of youthful girls, showing lots of leg and a high waist. Despite the preference in fashion for bold colors, many women continued to wear simple black dresses. This fun dress was worn by Joan Sheppard, who referred to it as her "car wash dress." The car wash style of dress, so named for its resemblance to automated car wash brushes, was made popular by Pierre Cardin in the 1960s.

Sleeveless crepe dress with floating panels, 1960s
Made by Petites by Suzy, New York
Gift of Joan Sheppard
2006 186 0042

Pauline Trigère

Paris-born Pauline Trigère moved to New York in 1937, at the age of twenty-five, to try working in the American fashion scene. In 1942 she opened her own fashion house, and she was producing ready-to-wear lines by the late 1940s. Trigère was known as a master cutter, creating crisp, structured, and tailored garments draped on a form or live model. This dress, worn by Lilly Christy Busch Hermann, is a perfect example of the work that Trigère was known for throughout her career; she was an innovator in her use of wool in dresses, jewelry attached to the dress, and a simple, yet tailored look. Her work is often descibed as timeless.

SLEEVELESS WOOL CREPE DRESS WITH
FAUX-JEWEL NECKLINE, CA. 1971
MADE BY PAULINE TRIGÈRE, NEW YORK
GIFT OF LOTSIE HOLTON
1995 022 0020

Pierre Cardin

Though Pierre Cardin is best known for his space-age designs and geometric shapes of the 1960s, the trend in 1970s design was greater simplicity as women generally wanted more comfortable clothing with fewer frills and details. This dress of heavyweight wool is an excellent example of this trend, with simple lines, minimal construction details, and a concealed zipper, allowing the wearer to dress it up or down with accessories.

Donor Mildred Topp-Othmer was the sister of Alice Topp-Lee, who designed junior-wear dresses for St. Louis company Doris Dodson. Mildred was a high school teacher and a buyer for her family's department store in Omaha before marrying Dr. Donald Othmer, an inventor and professor at the Polytechnic Institute of Brooklyn (now New York University Polytechnic School of Engineering). During their lifetime Mildred and Donald quietly amassed a fortune nearing $750 million, which they generously donated to many different organizations after their deaths. The Missouri Historical Society benefited from the generosity of "Mid" and her sister Alice with their donation of many high-end designer garments.

Long-sleeve wool dress, ca. 1973
Made by Pierre Cardin, Paris
Gift of Mildred Topp-Othmer
1976 071 0002

Clovis Ruffin

Designer Clovis Ruffin showed his first collection in 1972, and the next year he was the youngest recipient of the Coty American Fashion Critics' Award. His Ruffinwear line of clothing was mostly known for T-shirt dresses and casual knits, catering to younger women entering the workforce. This dress is a simple jersey wrap dress. The wrap dress, first made popular by designer Diane von Furstenberg, wraps around the body and ties, creating a deep V-neck. This style of dress became a symbol of women's liberation in the 1970s, with its comfort and ease of wear. Many women found that the wrap dress translated easily between work and social occasions.

This dress was worn by Mary-Randolph Dickson Ballinger, who attended Mary Institute and graduated from Washington University in St. Louis. She married Dr. Walter F. Ballinger II, who served as the head of the department of surgery at Washington University School of Medicine. Mary-Randolph worked in real estate, was the vice president of the board of the Missouri Historical Society, served on boards for many other civic organizations, and began running a cattle and horse ranch in Texas.

JERSEY-KNIT WRAP DRESS WITH RUFFLED
NECKLINE AND SLEEVES, CA. 1975
MADE BY CLOVIS RUFFIN, NEW YORK
GIFT OF MARY-RANDOLPH BALLINGER
1996 381 0003

Judy Caliendo

Women's clothing in the 1970s became far less formal. There was not a distinct look or silhouette that was appropriate for everyone because clothing was very experimental. Hippie attitudes about sexual expression and natural living, mixed with the feminist ideals of an equal society, led to a great shift in attitudes about clothing. Women generally wore what they felt comfortable in, and dresses came in fitted, loose, or oversize styles with skirts in mini, midi, and maxi lengths. This turtleneck midi-length dress is made of polyester, which became popular because it held up well and did not wrinkle. This was a draw to people looking for more modern conveniences.

DOUBLE-KNIT POLYESTER LONG-SLEEVE
DRESS WITH COWL COLLAR, CA. 1975
MADE BY JUDY CALIENDO FOR
TOGETHER, NEW YORK
GIFT OF PAULA WEPPRICH
1997 402 0001

Yves Saint Laurent

Yves Saint Laurent began his fashion career as a teenager, working for Christian Dior. He was named head of the House of Dior at just twenty-one years old upon Dior's death in 1957. His immediate and continued success made him one of the most influential designers of the twentieth century. In 1962 he opened his own fashion house with Pierre Berge, where he continued to influence the way women dressed, popularizing tuxedo suits for women, the safari look, and the beatnik look.

Often inspired by street wear, Saint Laurent created a line of peasant-style dresses in 1976. The peasant dress is characterized by a lower neckline, blousy sleeves, and a flowing skirt. While peasant dresses usually had more earthy patterns, this black version worn by Barbara Mahon is a more subtle and versatile take on the style. Mahon was a public relations director for Stix, Baer and Fuller in St. Louis for more than twenty years.

RAYON JERSEY KNIT PEASANT-STYLE
DRESS, CA. 1976
MADE BY YVES SAINT LAURENT, PARIS
GIFT OF BARBARA MAHON
1989 035 0004

The diversity of women's clothing styles that started in the 1970s continued on into the 1980s, with no clear lines of distinction for use with regard to day, work, or evening wear. Dresses came in all lengths and sizes, from loose and oversized to tight and fitted. This dress features the large shoulder pads prevalent in fashion through the 1980s. The draped and pleated skirt helps soften and feminize the look of the broad shoulders.

Kathryn Fulstone wore this dress for events such as a corporate party for KPLR-TV and her own twenty-fifth anniversary party. After obtaining her degree from University of Missouri–Columbia, she worked as both a teacher and an interior designer. Today she is a community leader, volunteering her time with many local nonprofit organizations.

SILK CREPE DRESS WITH GATHERED SKIRT,
1988
UNKNOWN MAKER
GIFT OF MR. AND MRS. ROBERT FULSTONE
2009 195 0006

A girl should be two things: classy and fabulous.

—Coco Chanel

Black at Night

Elegant, sophisticated, and powerful, the black evening dress is worn for more formal occasions. It can be almost any silhouette or length but is usually made of luxurious fabrics such as silk, velvet, or chiffon. Ornamentation, such as sequins, beads, fringe, and rhinestones, has also served to transform regular dresses into formal wear over the years.

In the 1920s, heavy beading and fringe exemplified the flapper-style evening wear. In the 1930s, designers such as Elsa Schiaparelli created long, lean, bias-cut evening gowns in black that hugged the body. In 1947, Christian Dior debuted his "New Look," transforming women's fashions into ultra-feminine fitted dresses with rounded shoulders, a tiny waist, and a full skirt. Dior preferred black, and he influenced designers around the world. In the 1960s, black evening wear competed with the popular psychedelic colors of the time, and styles evolved to be less constricting and more youthful. Exercise and disco influenced women's clothing in the 1970s as black evening wear began to once again hug the body. In the 1980s and 1990s, black dominated high fashion—and continues to do so today.

The flapper styles of the 1920s were easily identifiable as loose-fitting dresses with a drop waist, bare arms, and short skirts. This dress features apron-like panels at the front and back as well as fringe embellishment. Fringe was reserved for evening wear and was a popular feature on dresses worn while dancing. This dress was made by Madame Goodwin, presumably Ada J. Goodwin, a St. Louis dressmaker.

GEORGETTE DRESS WITH FRINGE TRIM,
CA. 1927
MADE BY MADAME GOODWIN, ST. LOUIS
GIFT OF MRS. TIMOTHY WILLIS
1994 062 0001

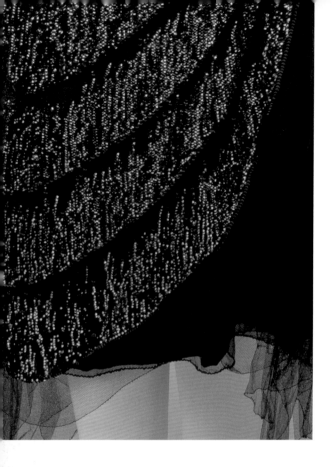

The Art Deco movement that began in the 1920s influenced all kinds of design, from buildings to everyday objects, with a sleek and modern style. Design elements such as geometric lines and abstract shapes were often used on clothing. This dress uses sequins to create straight and curved lines all over the dress. The gauzy fabric, heavy sequins, handkerchief hem, and hanging panels seen on this dress were all very common in evening wear throughout the 1920s.

SEQUINED EVENING DRESS, CA. 1927
UNKNOWN MAKER
GIFT OF MRS. GEORGE E. MELLOW
1960 083 0000

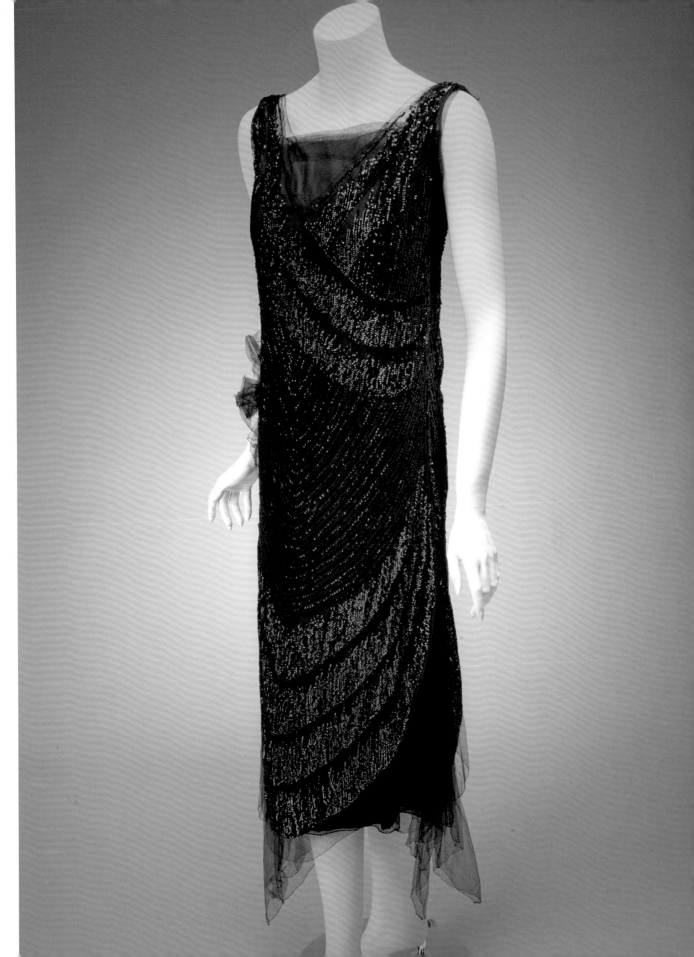

$\mathcal{T}$hough not attributed to any particular designer, the lace over-bodice style and uneven hem of this dress are very similar in design to the Chanel dress from the same time period (page 53), showing the influence that Parisian couture had over American fashion.

This dress was presumably worn by donor Henriette de Penaloza Schotten, daughter of Count Henri de Penaloza of Spain and heiress Marie Reine Fusz of Ferguson, Missouri. Marie went to finishing school in Paris, where Count Henri was working. The two met and returned to St. Louis to marry in 1897. Their daughter, Henriette, was born in St. Louis in 1903, just before her parents' divorce the following year. Henriette would have been in her early twenties when she wore this dress.

LACE EVENING DRESS WITH
RHINESTONE TRIM, CA. 1928
UNKNOWN MAKER
GIFT OF HENRIETTE DE PENALOZA
SCHOTTEN
1979 001 0009

*D*resses in the 1920s came in a variety of loose-fitting chemise styles that generally resembled a shapeless tube or barrel. The bloused, hip-wrapped style seen in this velvet dress from the 1920s is created by gathering the fabric above the dropped waistline. The design also includes a trompe l'oeil belt and bow at the waist. Trompe l'oeil is the illusion of a three-dimensional object created through design, in this case silver beads and rhinestones.

VELVET EVENING DRESS WITH
SILVER-BEAD AND RHINESTONE TRIM,
CA. 1928
MADE BY COHEN-JACKSON
GIFT OF MRS. FRANK M. MAYFIELD
1965 106 0001

109

$\mathcal{L}$otawana Flateau Nims wore this gown in the 1930s. The incredible detail and elegance of this dress suggests that it was for evening events or special occasions. Cape collars, as seen here, were popular at the time.

Lotawana was the wife of Eugene Dutton Nims, one of the founders of Pioneer Telephone and Telegraph Company (which became Southwestern Bell Telephone Company) and president of the company from 1919 to 1932. The couple married in 1914 and resided on Portland Place in St. Louis for more than sixty years. In 1929 the couple built a weekend home on their 192-acre estate, Bee Tree Farm, at the confluence of the Mississippi and Meramec rivers, and also maintained a summer home on Cape Cod. Bee Tree Park is now a St. Louis County park.

BIAS-CUT HALTER CREPE EVENING DRESS
WITH TURQUOISE BEADED CAPE COLLAR,
CA. 1932
UNKNOWN MAKER
GIFT OF MRS. EUGENE D. NIMS ESTATE
1966 032 0014

$\mathcal{T}$his gown was also worn by Lotawana Flateau Nims in the 1930s. It is made of crepe, a fabric popular in that decade for its ability to shape to the contours of the body when cut on the bias (diagonally). Slim evening dresses with bare backs and halter-style necklines were prevalent in the 1930s.

BIAS-CUT HALTER CREPE EVENING DRESS
WITH GREEN ACCENTS, CA. 1932–1935
MADE BY GOTTLIEB, NEW YORK
GIFT OF MRS. EUGENE D. NIMS ESTATE
1966 032 0015

Mainbocher

Main Rousseau Bocher was an American designer who worked in Paris from 1929 to 1939 and returned the United States to reopen his salon in New York during World War II, where he stayed until 1971. He made expensive couture dresses for high-end clients and was known for uncomplicated designs that were elegant and chic. In the 1930s he made simple bias-cut, slip-style evening dresses with shoulder bows and godets (triangular panels) in the skirt.

This dress belonged to Mary Elizabeth Lumaghi, who married James Marsh Douglas in 1939. After living in Jefferson City, the family returned to St. Louis in 1949. Mary enjoyed being a housewife and mother, as well as a gracious hostess to those in the legal and political communities.

BIAS-CUT CREPE EVENING DRESS WITH
SPAGHETTI STRAPS, CA. 1933
MADE BY MAINBOCHER, PARIS
GIFT OF JAMES KIMBALL DOUGLAS
1975 005 0004

Elsa Schiaparelli

Italian fashion designer Elsa Schiaparelli moved to Paris to become a couturier in the 1920s. Considered Coco Chanel's biggest rival, she launched a collection of knitwear in 1927, quickly adding additional items including evening wear in 1931. Known for her creative fashions and surrealist influences, Schiaparelli collaborated with famous artists like Salvador Dalí to create some of her most unusual and innovative designs. She used the color black frequently, believing that every woman should own a black dress and a black suit. Her work is often described as genius.

In addition to creative use of zippers, bold colors, and humorous prints, Schiaparelli was also known for bias-cut evening dresses. This dress, worn by Mary Elizabeth Lumaghi, is an excellent example of Schiaparelli's innovation and creativity. In addition to the bias cut, the dress features an extra piece of fabric that drapes from the chest and can be wrapped around the waist to form a belt.

SILK BIAS-CUT EVENING DRESS, CA. 1933
MADE BY SCHIAPARELLI, PARIS
GIFT OF JAMES KIMBALL DOUGLAS
1975 005 0000

The design of this dress is indicative of the style of the early 1940s: square, padded shoulders; a nipped, belted waistline; and a gathered skirt. The floor-length hem and the appearance of a modified day dress were common for evening wear, particularly during the war years.

This dress was worn by Elizabeth Chapin Carson, wife of William Glasgow Bruce Carson, a professor of English who specialized in playwriting and theater history at Washington University in St. Louis from 1919 to 1957. Elizabeth attended Washington University and was a member of the board of managers of the Mission Free School of St. Louis, a home for poor, abused, or homeless children located in what is now Webster Groves.

MATTE CREPE EVENING DRESS WITH
GOLD METAL TRIM AND BELT, CA. 1940
UNKNOWN MAKER
GIFT OF MRS. WILLIAM C. CARSON
1983 089 0002

$\mathcal{D}$orothea Davies Meier wore this elegant sequined evening gown in the 1940s while onboard the RMS *Queen Mary*. The ship sailed weekly for a transatlantic trip between Southampton, England, and New York City.

Dorothea was born in 1900 and married Arthur John Meier in 1922. Arthur worked for the family business, Meier & Pohlmann Furniture Company, while Dorothea stayed home with their three children. The couple traveled extensively, frequently on cruises, where formal attire was required for onboard evening dining. Dorothea was described by her granddaughter as "always impeccably dressed, accessorized, manicured, and coiffed."

CHIFFON AND SEQUIN EVENING DRESS,
CA. 1940
UNKNOWN MAKER
GIFT OF MRS. M. CATHERINE
UNDERHILL FITZPATRICK
2009 188 0007

Ceil Chapman

Ceil Chapman, who received the Coty American Fashion Critics' Award in 1945, specialized in cocktail and formal dresses. Like Norman Norell, Chapman was able to sucessfully adapt Christian Dior's "New Look" style for American audiences. Often described as an engineer, Chapman was adept at draping fabrics to create her signature styles. This dress uses gores to create a flared, wrapped skirt with rounded edges and a bow, all of which are lined with pink satin for a dramatic touch.

SATIN EVENING DRESS WITH
PINK LINING, 1950s
MADE BY CEIL CHAPMAN, NEW YORK
GIFT OF STEVEN AND HELEN
MARAVICH ESTATE
1998 300 0006

$\mathcal{W}$hile many dresses in the 1950s featured a large full skirt, a slimmer silhouette was also popular at the time. This dress, worn by Emilie Brandhorst, features a belted bodice and a tiered skirt that would accentuate the wearer's waist and hips. The silhouette of this dress made it appropriate for a cocktail dress, while the rhinestones helped to transition it into evening wear. Emilie Brandhorst was an honorary member of the Women's Club of Washington University in St. Louis, where her husband, Dr. William S. Brandhorst, was on the faculty at the School of Dentistry.

SLEEVELESS CREPE COCKTAIL DRESS WITH
TIERED SKIRT AND RHINESTONE TRIM,
CA. 1955
UNKNOWN MAKER
GIFT OF MRS. EMILIE BRANDHORST
2002 139 0007

Saks Fifth Avenue

The appearance of soft shoulders, cinched waists, and full skirts began with Christian Dior's "New Look" in 1947 and continued to grow in popularity throughout the 1950s. Made for retailer Saks Fifth Avenue, this dress exemplifies that hourglass silhouette and uses a large faille bow and built-in petticoats to increase the fullness of the skirt while also decreasing the size of the waist.

This dress was worn by Gertrude "Gee Gee" Bland Platt. Gee Gee attended Mary Institute, followed by Connecticut College for Women, where she studied history, English, and economics. She became a preservation activist in San Francisco, where she has positively impacted the existence of well-known landmarks, monuments, and buildings.

VELVET EVENING DRESS WITH LARGE
FAILLE BOW, CA. 1955
MADE FOR SAKS FIFTH AVENUE
GIFT OF GERTRUDE BLAND PLATT
2003 106 0012

Bergdorf Goodman

The ultra-feminine fashions of the 1950s are reflected in this black lace strapless dress. Strapless dresses first appeared in the 1930s and gained in popularity throughout the 1940s and 1950s. This dress is made of layers of lace draped horizontally across the body, and a stiff taffeta lining helps keep its shape. Purchased at high-end New York retailer Bergdorf Goodman, this evening dress was custom made for Mary Elizabeth Bascom in 1957. Bascom was the granddaughter of Joseph D. Bascom, co-founder of the Broderick and Bascom Rope Company in St. Louis. She traveled extensively and volunteered her time at many cultural institutions throughout St. Louis, including the Saint Louis Zoo, Missouri Botanical Garden, and Missouri Historical Society.

Strapless lace dress, 1957
Purchased at Bergdorf Goodman,
New York
Gift of Mary Elizabeth Bascom
1978 001 0002

Christian Dior

When Christian Dior debuted his "New Look" in 1947 it met with great success. Women were tired of wartime restrictions and ready for more feminine styles. Known for tiny waists and full swinging skirts, Dior ruled the fashion world for the next ten years until his death at age fifty-seven. In 1960, Marc Bohan took over as head designer for the House of Dior and presented his first collection in 1961, showing his "Slim Look."

This sleeveless cocktail dress dates to around 1961 and has a straight bodice with a boned bra inside to help give the proper silhouette. The dress appears to be constructed in two pieces, but is just a slim skirt with a deep inverted pleat, giving the illusion of a double skirt.

SLEEVELESS COCKTAIL DRESS WITH
PATTERN OF CUT VELVET DOTS
AND VELVET BOW, CA. 1961
MADE BY CHRISTIAN DIOR, PARIS
GIFT OF MILDRED TOPP-OTHMER
1977 136 0000

Vera Hicks

Starting her own dress-making business in St. Louis in 1929 at the age of seventeen, Vera Hicks, along with her mother, worked under the name of Hicks and Hicks. Ten years later, the shop was bought out by the department store Scruggs-Vandervoort-Barney, and Vera and her mother were relocated to a dress-making salon on the eighth floor of Scruggs, where they worked for several years. It was there that Vera made a name for herself creating custom designs for local notables, queen and special maid gowns for the Veiled Prophet Ball, and garments for leading women throughout the country. In 1956 Vera Hicks left Scruggs and opened her own shop at the Park Plaza Hotel, where she worked for another seventeen years until her retirement.

Hicks based her styles on a model of simplicity. She was often quoted for emphasizing the importance of fashion as a physical embodiment of the wearer's personality. She believed clothing should not overpower a woman or impede her lifestyle. Hicks was known for focusing on originality in her creations and took time to become acquainted with her customers, to ensure her design would fit their personalities. This simple black jersey knit dress is an excellent example of Hicks's simple yet elegant style and makes it easy to see why owner Mary Hudson Jones made it onto a St. Louis "best dressed list."

BLACK JERSEY-KNIT DRESS WITH LONG
SLEEVES AND TURTLENECK, CA. 1969
MADE BY VERA HICKS, ST. LOUIS
GIFT OF MR. AND MRS. JAMES HUDSON JONES
1976 023 0013

Halston

You can't talk about fashion in the 1970s without mentioning Halston. Roy Halston Frowick (known simply as Halston) began designing millinery in the 1950s, adding a line of women's clothing in 1966. Known for working with fabrics such as jersey and ultra-suede, he reinvented simple pieces like the shirtwaist dress and the caftan. In 1972, *Newsweek* named him the "the premier fashion designer of all America."

Among Halston's signature looks was this iconic jersey-knit halter dress that gave women an elongated silhouette. Halston dressed an elite clientele of movie stars and society women during the days of disco and Studio 54. This simple yet stylish dress exemplifies Halston's design aesthetic—easy and without excess, sexy but still elegant.

JERSEY HALTER DRESS, CA. 1974
MADE BY HALSTON, NEW YORK
GIFT OF BARBARA MAHON
1989 035 0003

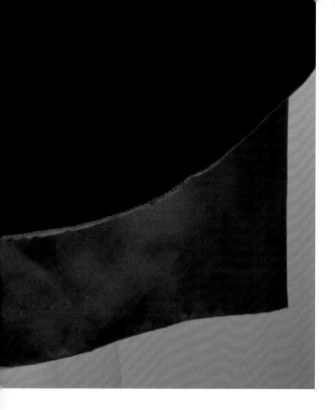

Pierre Cardin

Pierre Cardin began his fashion career at the age of fourteen, working as an apprentice. He moved from Italy to Paris in 1945 and worked with designers like Schiaparelli and Dior before opening his own house in 1950. Inventor of the "bubble dress," he is known for using sharp angles and geometric shapes, as well as futuristic design, throughout his career.

Barbara Mahon wore this dress to cocktail parties and dinners in the late 1970s. The velvet and heavy satin in this dress make it more appropriate for evening wear. Mahon worked in advertising and public relations for several prominent St. Louis companies throughout her career.

VELVET TUNIC-STYLE DRESS WITH HEAVY
SATIN UNDERSKIRT, CA. 1975
MADE BY PIERRE CARDIN, PARIS
GIFT OF BARBARA MAHON
1989 035 0005

Geoffrey Beene

In 1988, *Vogue* magazine called fashion designer Geoffrey Beene "the most original, idiosyncratic, autonomous creator in his field," a field over which he reigned in the 1970s and 1980s. In the 1970s, Beene was inspired to make lighter and more fluid pieces, as well as use less expensive fabrics for evening wear, like this jersey-knit dress. The unusual pink and green ribbon trim showcases his originality and artistic skill.

BLACK JERSEY SHEATH DRESS WITH
PINK RIBBON TRIM, CA. 1975
MADE BY GEOFFREY BEENE, NEW YORK
GIFT OF EUGENE M. REESE
1992 018 0007

Dianne Hopkins

Dianne Hopkins was a fashion design student at Washington University in St. Louis when she made this dress for a class project in 1976. After graduation she worked as an assistant designer in New York for two years before returning to St. Louis to start a business of her own specializing in wedding dresses and gowns for the Veiled Prophet and Fleur de Lis balls.

While the red-satin-lined fringe on this dress is reminiscent of the "modern" flapper girls of the 1920s, the plunging neckline speaks to the modern woman of the 1970s and the freedom of expression many women were experiencing during the sexual revolution.

Double-knit polyester dress with
red-satin-lined fringe, 1976
Made by Mrs. Dianne Hopkins,
St. Louis
Gift of Mrs. Dianne Hopkins Wilcox
1997 354 0002

Bill Blass

Bill Blass began his career as a fashion designer at age fifteen, when he would sell sketches of his designs to a New York manufacturer from his home in Indiana. After serving during World War II, Blass moved to New York to begin his career. In 1959 he began working at Maurice Renter, a company he would buy out and rename Bill Blass, Inc., in 1970. Blass was known for both his tailored classic pieces and his evening gowns. This one-shoulder dress worn by Lilly Christy Busch Hermann features ostrich feathers, a trim that Blass used with some frequency.

ONE-SHOULDER DRESS WITH OSTRICH
FEATHER TRIM, CA. 1980
MADE BY BILL BLASS, NEW YORK
GIFT OF LOTSIE HOLTON
1995 022 0007

Oscar de la Renta

Oscar de la Renta was born in the Dominican Republic in 1932. At age eighteen he left the Caribbean to study painting in Madrid. His interest in fashion design quickly grew, and he began an apprenticeship with Cristóbal Balenciaga. In 1961 he began working for Lanvin-Castillo, and within two years he'd moved to New York to work for Elizabeth Arden, through 1965. He then moved to Jane Derby as head designer before buying the company and changing it to his own label. In 1973 he founded Oscar de la Renta Couture. In 1975, *Vogue* magazine declared him the "King of Evening." His clothing lines were known for being feminine and romantic, often having a Latin feel.

This fitted mermaid-style dress was worn by Lilly Christy Busch Hermann, the oldest daughter of Marie Christy Busch and August A. "Gussie" Busch, head of Anheuser-Busch. Hermann was active in the Junior League and Muscular Dystrophy Association in St. Louis and formed the Lilly Christy Busch Hermann Foundation to benefit local charities. This dress is an excellent representation of 1980s evening wear with its sequins and tiered polka-dot skirt.

STRAPLESS SEQUINED LACE AND NET DRESS,
CA. 1982
MADE BY OSCAR DE LA RENTA, NEW YORK
GIFT OF LOTSIE HOLTON
1995 022 0008

Morton Myles

Morton Myles gained success as a designer when Jacqueline Kennedy wore one of his designs on the cover of *Look* magazine in 1961. Throughout the years he stayed true to his belief that "clothes should enhance the body and should not only cover defects but should do something for the psyche" (Polly Rayner, "Designer Morton Myles Believes in Silhouettes That Flatter Women," *The Morning* [PA] *Call*, April 14, 1985). His main goal was to flatter the feminine form. In the 1980s Myles designed his black dresses, what he referred to as his "social clothes," to stylishly fall just below the knee.

While Myles believed that clothes should not be so trendy that they wouldn't be wearable for very long, the broad shoulders and giant ruffled sleeves on this dress definitely reflect the 1980s era in which it was made.

SHIFT DRESS WITH LARGE RUFFLED SLEEVES,
CA. 1984
MADE BY MORTON MYLES FOR THE WARRENS,
NEW YORK
GIFT OF MARY DEBRECHT
2000 203 0005

The influence of sports on fashion began as early as the 1920s but really began to mix with mainstream fashions in the 1980s. This rayon halter dress is made in a racerback style, a design that originated with swimwear. The racerback first appeared in women's clothing in the 1960s and 1970s before coming around again in the 1990s. Donor Amy Berra wore this dress to a New Year's Eve party in 1991.

Sleeveless rayon dress with halter-style bodice into racerback, 1991
Made by Shox Clothing, Inc., Los Angeles
Gift of Amy Berra
2006 141 0004

$\mathcal{B}$y the 1990s the rules of appropriate dress (which had been loosening for decades) were somewhat nonexistent as styles became more varied and the lines between clothing categories (i.e., day wear, work wear, evening wear) became blurred. Worn to a high school prom in 1992, this dress may not have been thought suitable in previous decades for its short style or its color, as black was not always considered appropriate for younger girls and teenagers to wear. The color black was slowly pushed to the forefront of youth fashion with the beatniks in the 1950s and 1960s, the punk movement in the 1970s and 1980s, and the grunge movement that began in the early 1990s.

RAYON AND POLYESTER LACE HALTER
DRESS, 1992
MADE BY JOANN SIMON FOR JUMP,
NEW YORK
COURTESY OF SHANNON MEYER
L2015 024 0001

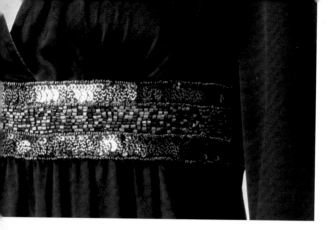

Kimora Lee Simmons

Designer Kimora Lee Simmons was born in St. Louis in 1975. Her half-Japanese and half–African American heritage, unique features, and five-foot, ten-inch stature set her apart when she began modeling at a young age. At age fourteen she moved to Paris to model for Chanel, having caught the eye of designer Karl Lagerfeld.

Simmons served as Lagerfeld's muse and the face of Chanel for two seasons, representing the embodiment of the 1990s. Back and forth between St. Louis and Paris, she managed to eventually graduate from Lutheran North High School. From 1998 to 2009, she was married to mogul Russell Simmons, co-founder of Def Jam records and the Phat Farm clothing company, which led to her role as CEO and creative director of the Baby Phat children's clothing line from 2002 to 2010.

Simmons's own clothing line made its official debut in December 2014 as KLS Kimora Lee Simmons. This simple black silk dress with a deep V-neck, bishop sleeves, and attached sequin belt creating an empire waist represents her evolution as a designer, showing practicality, sophistication, and versatility.

SILK DRESS WITH BISHOP SLEEVES AND
EMPIRE WAIST, CA. 2014
MADE BY KLS KIMORA LEE SIMMONS,
NEW YORK
8320

Michael Drummond

St. Louis designer Michael Drummond grew up in North County and graduated from McCluer High School in 1998. He attended the Academy of Art College (now University) in San Francisco, where he studied knitwear design. He soon began his own label, Exquisite Corpse. In 2010 he was selected to appear on the eighth season of the televised reality design show *Project Runway*, where he gained much national and international recognition. After the show, he returned to St. Louis to continue to introduce new designs and work with local institutions, such as the Regional Arts Commission, to promote fashion within the city.

Drummond has a unique design aesthetic, wanting his pieces "to be easy and effortless without sacrificing the edginess and quality that is the cornerstone of the line" (Sarah Stallmann, "Michael Drummond Hosts Showroom Grand Opening," *ALIVE* Style Notes blog, July 10, 2014).

This dress features his signature knitwear combined with repurposed x-rays. It was worn by Elizabeth Tucker, CEO and co-founder of ALIVE Media Group, which produces *ALIVE* magazine and the annual Saint Louis Fashion Week. She wore this dress to the *A Queen Within* exhibit gala at the World Chess Hall of Fame in 2014.

KNIT AND X-RAY DRESS, 2014
MADE BY MICHAEL DRUMMOND,
ST. LOUIS
COURTESY OF ELIZABETH TUCKER
L2015 009 0001

Enzoani

The rules associated with wearing a black dress have certainly evolved. We still wear black to funerals, but now women even wear black to weddings—including the bride. To some the color black might seem too nontraditional, too sexy, or too somber for a wedding dress—the antithesis of such a joyous occasion. Throughout the nineteenth and early twentieth centuries women generally avoided wearing black to their weddings. An old wives' tale even discouraged the wearing of black: "Married in black, you'll wish yourself back." If a death occurred near the time of a wedding some brides did wear black, but women were allowed to relax the rules of mourning etiquette for their wedding day. Gowns of white or gray were acceptable, as long as embellishments and veils remained modest. As mourning etiquette subsided, women found ways of incorporating black into their nuptial wardrobes. Throughout the twentieth century women had occasion to wear black on their wedding day, particularly during the Depression and war years, when a best dress or suit was all that was affordable.

In 2012, Vera Wang created a line of black wedding dresses, setting the stage for black as the hot color in bridal wear. This dress is made by Enzoani, a company focusing on "cutting edge" design in bridal wear. Made in a mermaid style, it incorporates a lightly colored underdress with black lace on a tulle overlay.

WEDDING DRESS, 2014
MADE BY ENZOANI, TUSTIN, CA
ANONYMOUS GIFT
2015 134 0001

It is tiresome everlasting to wear black, but nothing is so serviceable, nothing so unrecognizable, nothing looks so well on every occasion.

—Emily Post

Resources

Arenson, Karen W. "Staggering Bequests by Unassuming Couple." *New York Times*, July 13, 1998. http://www.nytimes.com/1998/07/13/nyregion/staggering-bequests-by-unassuming-couple.html?pagewanted=all.

Brett, Mary. *Fashionable Mourning Jewelry, Clothing & Customs*. Atglen, PA: Schiffer, 2006.

Campbell, Mark. *The Art of Hair Work*. Edited by Jules & Kaethe Kliot. Berkeley, CA: Lacis Publications, 1875, 1989.

Cunnington, C. Willett. *Fashion and Women's Attitudes in the Nineteenth Century*. Mineola, NY: Dover Publications, 2003.

Davey, Richard. *A History of Mourning*. London: McCorquodale, 1890. http://publicdomainreview.org/collections/a-history-of-mourning-1890/.

Eaton, Phoebe. "Kimora Lee Simmons, the New Queen of Conspicuous Consumption." *New York Times*, June 21, 2004. http://nymag.com/nymetro/shopping/fashion/features/9306/.

Fivel, Sharon. *From Carriage Trade to Ready-Made: St. Louis Clothing Designers, 1880-1920*. St. Louis: Missouri Historical Society Press, 1992.

Flower, Margaret. *Victorian Jewellery*. South Brunswick, NJ: A. S. Barnes, 1967.

Fukai, Akiko. *Fashion: The Collection of the Kyoto Costume Institute*. Cologne, Germany: Taschen, 2002.

Hollander, Anne, et al. *In Black and White: Dress from the 1920s to Today*. Columbus: Wexner Center for the Arts, Ohio State University, 1992.

Loughridge, Patricia R. and Edward D. C. Campbell, Jr. *Women in Mourning*. Richmond, Virginia: The Museum of the Confederacy, 1985.

Ludot, Didier. *The Little Black Dress: Vintage Treasure*. New York: Assouline, 2001.

Mendes, Valerie. *Dressed in Black*. London: V&A Publications, 1999.

Muyco-Tobin, Trish. "Family Ties: The Ladue News Show House." *Ladue News*, October 17, 2013.

Payne, Blanche, Geitel Winako, and Jane Farrell-Beck. *The History of Costume*. New York: HarperCollins, 1992.

Pike, Martha V., and Janice Gray Armstrong. *A Time To Mourn: Expressions of Grief in Nineteenth Century America*. Stony Brook, NY: The Museums at Stony Brook, 1980.

Post, Emily. *Etiquette in Society, in Business, in Politics and at Home*. New York: Funk & Wagnalls, 1922. Online version: https://books.google.com/books?id=HhAYAAAAIAAJ.

Rayner, Polly. "Designer Morton Myles Believes in Silhouettes That Flatter Women." *The Morning* [PA] *Call*, April 14, 1985. Online version: http://articles.mcall.com/1985-04-14/features/2476853_1_dress-preppy-flounces.

Stallman, Sarah. "Michael Drummond Hosts Showroom Grand Opening." *Alive* Magazine, July 10, 2014. http://www.alivemag.com/blog/index.php/2014/07/michael-drummond-hosts-showroom-grand-opening/.

Steele, Valerie. *The Black Dress*. New York: HarperCollins, 2007.

Taylor, Lou. *Mourning Dress: A Costume and Social History*. London: G. Allen and Unwin, 1983.

Vogue Magazine. "Voguepedia." Accessed 2014. http://www.vogue.com.